Developed and produced by Ripley Publishing Ltd

This edition published and distributed by:
Mason Crest Publishers Inc.
370 Reed Road, Broomall, Pennsylvania 19008
(866) MCP-BOOK (toll free)
www.masoncrest.com

Ripley's Believe It or Not!
Totally Obsessed
ISBN 978-1-4222-1541-8
Library of Congress Cataloging-in-Publication data is available

Ripley's Believe It or Not!—Complete 16 Title Series
ISBN 978-1-4222-1529-6

PUBLISHER'S NOTE
While every effort has been made to verify the accuracy of the entries in this book,
the Publishers cannot be held responsible for any errors contained in the work.
They would be glad to receive any information from readers.

WARNING
Some of the stunts and activities in this book are undertaken by experts and should not
be attempted by anyone without adequate training and supervision.

Printed in the United States of America

PUBLISHING

a Jim Pattison Company

Totally Obsessed

The more the merrier! Clothes Pin Man

demonstrates there's more than one use for

that handy wooden peg. The baseball that's

had so many coats of paint it's got its own

bedroom and the lady who can spin 100

hula-hoops at one time.

Competitive eater Crazy Legs Conti eats
his way out of a popcorn sarcophagus...

GrEAt BaLL of PaiNt

Mike Carmichael accepts requests from total strangers to have a layer of the ball painted in their honor. He often paints their name or message on the ball.

EVERY DAY SINCE 1977, house painter Mike Carmichael of Alexandria, Indiana, has applied at least one coat of paint to a regulation baseball.

More than 21,400 coats of paint later, the initial 9-in (23-cm) circumference has ballooned to more than 126 in (320 cm), and the weight of the ball has increased to 2,700 lbs (1,224 kg) making it the world's largest ball of paint. Mike lets a guest of honor paint every hundredth coat, and has kept detailed records of the many colors of the ball's layers. The ball has now grown so big that he has had to build a special room in his house just to store it. The attraction has drawn many visitors, some from as far away as Thailand.

Twine Passions

Francis A. Johnson's efforts (top right) inspired Frank Stoeber of Cawker City, Kansas, who managed to roll over 1,600,000 ft (487,680 m) of twine into a sphere 11 ft (3 m) in diameter. But just when he seemed certain to overtake his Darwin rival, Stoeber died. The Cawker City ball then became a community project, but Johnson's supporters dismiss its superiority because it became the work of more than one man.

Close to the Wire

"Clonia," created by Lyle Lynch of Phoenix, Arizona, was the biggest barbed-wire ball in the world from 1970 until the late 1990s. With a diameter of 80 in (2 m) and a weight of more than 5,000 lb (2,268 kg), it consists of 16 mi (26 km) of wire!

Stringing us Along

For years Francis A. Johnson spent his lunch hour painstakingly wrapping twine on his farm in Darwin, Minnesota. When he died in 1989, the ball measured 12 ft (4 m) in diameter and weighed 17,400 lbs (7,892 kg).

Let's Stick Together

Boys Town, Nebraska, is home to the world's largest ball of stamps. The ball, which weighs in at 600 lb (272 kg), is housed in the town's Philamatic Museum. It was pasted together by the local stamp-collecting club over the course of six months in the early 1950s. Why did the philatelists get so stuck in? "It must have been an exceptionally cold winter," says the museum's director.

First-class Effort

In the 1930s, postmaster Virden Graham of Indiana completed a 130-lb (59-kg) ball of brown cotton string that he had taken from first-class bundles. It took him 16 years, and the ball consisted of an impressive 78 mi (126 km) of string.

Ball Room

Weighing more than 6 tons and measuring 41 in (104 cm) wide, this ball was created by J.C. Payne of Texas to beat the previous world's biggest ball of binder twine, the Darwin Ball.

Ripley's®

GIANT BALL OF TWINE
EXHIBIT NO: 10787
THIS GIANT BALL OF TWINE MEASURES
42 IN (107 CM) IN CIRCUMFERENCE

To Cap it All

Over a period of 30 years, Emanuele "Litto" Damonte (1892–1985), the "Hubcap King" of Pope Valley, California, collected more than 2,000 vehicle hubcaps.

Hubcap in Hand

Known as the "Hubcap Queen," Lucy Pearson of the U.S. has a collection of more than 200,000 hubcaps!

Foul Play

Eighty-three-year-old Abe Coleman of Tacoma, Washington, has a penchant for catching foul balls. For the past two decades, the sprightly octogenarian has stood in the parking lot of the town's minor-league ballpark during every game, complete with baseball glove in hand, running back and forth in hot pursuit of all those errant baseballs. When one really goes astray, he has even been known to crawl under parked cars to retrieve it.

That's a Record

In the 1960s and 1970s, a Washington, D.C. man known as "Mingering Mike" created fake long-playing records. Each album, complete with a hand-illustrated cover, full liner notes, lyric sheets, a bar code, and even a cardboard "record," was designed with painstaking detail—some of them were even shrink-wrapped! Thirty-eight of the convincing fakes were discovered at a flea market as recently as 2004.

TOP FIVE
MOST COMMON OBSESSIONS

1 Fear of contamination

2 Fear of causing harm to someone else

3 Fear of making mistakes

4 Fear of behaving in a way that is socially unacceptable

5 Need for exactness

If the Hubcap Fits...

Sculptor Ptolemy Elrington of Brighton, England, recycles old hubcaps into sculptures, mostly of fish, "to try to say things about our wasteful society."

Split Personality

England's Alfred West holds the world record for splitting hairs—he split a human hair into 18 parts, making all the cuts from one point.

Habit-forming

Statistics compiled by the Obsessive Compulsive Foundation suggest that as many as one in 50 adults in the United States suffers from Obsessive Compulsive Disorder. These sufferers become obsessed by doubts or worries to the point where their lives become disrupted. They often feel compelled to perform certain actions—for example, repeated hand-washing, arranging, counting, collecting, and hoarding—in order to alleviate their distress.

The Little Top

Roll up for the smallest show on earth! Paul Tandy from Warwick, England, has spent the last nine years creating a model circus, with miniature animals, and more than 500 entertainers. Inspired by a visit to the circus when Paul was ten, P.J. Tandy's International Circus is accurate in every detail, down to a cannon, which fires a mini human cannon ball, and tiny elephant droppings.

Stub it Out

Since 2001, anti-smoking activist Zhang Yue has attempted to convert China's 350 million smokers—one by one. Traveling around the country, he approaches smokers and tries to convince them to quit. He will even buy their cigarettes from them.

Swat Team

After a fly wrecked a lucrative deal by landing in a client's meal, Chinese businessman Hu Xilin vowed revenge. That was ten years ago, and since then Hu says that he has killed 88 lbs (40 kg) of flies and can identify 25 different species.

On the House

When John F. Kennedy was still president, John Zweifel decided to build a miniature version of the White House. Forty years later, the 60 ft (18 m) by 20 ft (6 m) replica has a place of honor at Zweifel's House of Presidents in Clermont, Florida. On a scale of one inch to one foot, the model mirrors the real thing right down to cracks in the walls and coffee stains on the rugs. There are lights in every room, the toilets flush, and there is even a tiny working TV in the West Wing. John sees only one problem with his fiddly miniature White House: "If a light goes out on a chandelier, it could take more than 16 hours to change it."

Chinese Tea

Twelfth-century Chinese Emperor Hui Tsung drank tea, wrote about tea, held tea-identifying competitions, and had teahouses built. His tea obsession was so great that he hardly noticed when his empire was overthrown by the Monguls.

Open House

Joseph Peterson of Cloquet, Minnesota, collects presidential and first lady memorabilia. His filing cabinets, full of material, include Christmas cards from the White House, and pictures of presidential dogs. He has shaken hands with every president since Gerald Ford, apart from Ronald Reagan.

Dish the Dirt

Glenn Johanson collects dirt from all around the world and proudly displays it in glass vials in his Museum of Dirt in Boston.

Barefaced Cheeks

In January 2004, British rambler Stephen Gould achieved his ambition of completing a 1,000-mi (1,600-km) walk—naked. He was arrested several times along the way and served two jail sentences.

Totally Nuts

Elizabeth Tashjian is nuts about nuts. Known as "The Nut Lady," Elizabeth, an accomplished artist, has been fascinated with the fruit since she thought she saw a human face in a Brazil nut in 1938. She then opened a Nut Museum in Old Lyme, Connecticut, and even performed a song about nuts on *The Tonight Show Starring Johnny Carson*. Until it closed in 2002, the museum housed all manner of nutty artifacts—nutcrackers, nut masks, nut sculptures, and the world's largest nut, a 35-pounder from the Seychelles.

The Name of the Game

A massive fan of the games console, John Sterling actually changed his name by law to Sony PlayStation!

Cartoon Capers

GEORGE C. REIGER JR., a Pennsylvania postal worker, is goofy about Disney characters.

The 51-year-old has more than 1,650 Disney tattoos from the base of his neck to the tops of his toes. His first cartoon tattoo was Mickey Mouse on his forearm. Now the whale from *Pinocchio* (US 1940) yawns on his belly, Beauty and the Beast dance on his left shoulder, and Alice in Wonderland fills his upper arm. On his back are 103 Dalmatians—his tattoo artist got carried away!

George spends $50,000 a year on his Disney habit and has even spent all six of his Honeymoons at Disney World in Florida.

George Reiger also owns more than 19,500 Disney collectibles and lives in a custom-built, Disney-themed house.

Taking the Mickey

Benji Breitbart is so mad about all things Disney that he spends six days a week at Disneyland, California. He knows the entire history of the park, dresses almost exclusively in Disney clothes, and refers to Disney as "we" even though he doesn't work for the corporation.

All Mixed Up

An Englishman who gave up trainspotting as it was too boring now has more than 1,000 pictures of cement-mixers. Ronnie Crossland, of Yorkshire, first developed his passion after spotting a new mixer being delivered to a building site in 1987. He has since traveled more than 200,000 mi (322,000 km) taking photos of cement-mixers, which he describes as "things of incredible beauty."

Skater Mom

Barbara Ordonaka can't seem to outgrow her childhood preoccupation with skateboarding. When she isn't skating around her house in Orange County, California, she is busy running the International Society of Skateboarding Moms, or using her skateboard to distribute books to needy children, or promoting her book, which is titled… you guessed it, *Skateboard Mom.*

Get Set, Go

Jane Withers, a child star of Hollywood films of the 1930s and 1940s, has a collection of showbiz memorabilia large enough to fill a warehouse. Her stash of more than 42,000 items includes parts of TV and movie sets, costumes, dolls, and scripts.

Praise the Gourd

Marvin Johnson could never get enough gourds. He and his wife Mary had so many of the strange-looking vegetables at their house in Angier, North Carolina, that they set up a Gourd Museum in 1965. The exhibits are mostly of gourd art. There is a gourd xylophone, a gourd Popeye, and a menagerie of gourd animals. "I've made lots of friends through gourds," Marvin once said.

The Best Possible Paste

Dr. Valkopolkov of Saginaw, Michigan, has collected more than 800 tubes of toothpaste from around the world, including such exotic flavors as tuna and Scotch.

Double-blind Test

Frank Keith of Illinois, could write backward, upside-down, and blind-folded! He could also simultaneously write any name or phrase with his left hand in front and his right hand behind.

The Write Stuff

Zelma George, of Canton, Ohio, had an amazing ability—not only could she write both forward and backward, she could also write upside down and upside down backward!

The Hole Story

The world's most pierced woman, Brazilian Elaine Davidson, puts her finger through her pierced tongue! So far she has 1,903 body piercings. Elaine has also been known to walk on beds of fire, broken glass, and nails. For her next feat: she wants to exceed 2,000 piercings!

Is it a Bird, Is it a Plane...

Native Californian John Ninomiya is one of only a few cluster balloonists in the world. He and his crew tie between 50 and 150 latex balloons on to a harness… and up and away he goes. So far, he has made about two dozen flights.

Duck and Cover

Nancy Townsend is so obsessed with her pet ducks and geese that she has invented diapers for them so that they can live indoors. Nancy dresses as Mother Goose, and is often seen taking her birds for walks on a leash.

Mac Attack

Computer technician Andrew Dusing makes furniture out of old Macintosh computer boxes and their Styrofoam inserts. His New York apartment is furnished with his recycled creations: A sofa, a dining table, a set of chairs, and CD racks. His ambition is to one day make a '57 Chevy.

Hearse Case Scenario

Rachel Ellam-Lloyd was so obsessed with vampires that she used to drive her young daughter to school in London in a 23-ft (7-m) long hearse. Little Georgina sat in the back where the coffin should be. Rachel also used the hearse—bought for her by her husband—to go shopping and to attend meetings of the Vampire Connections group.

A Sick Sense of Humor

Steve Dixon has been collecting airline sick-bags for 23 years. In that time he has amassed a collection of more than 180 bags.

Blood Brothers

Grab a bite with local vampires on International Vampire Meetup Day. Once a month, thousands of aspiring bloodsuckers meet at an appointed time in more than 650 different locations around the world. The most popular cities for meetups are London, followed by New York City, and Houston, Texas.

BEAM ME UP?

STAR TREK FANS Mikel and Craig Salsgiver displayed the Vulcan greeting as they renewed their marriage vows on the Starship Enterprise.

Who would have Guest?

Miosav Static has attended more than 1,500 weddings in western Serbia… without ever being invited! Miosav, who finds out the times and locations from the local media, says he loves the atmosphere and food at weddings. He doesn't expect something for nothing, however, and always takes a present for the bride.

The Salsgivers were among four couples to be selected to take part in the "Intergalactic Weddings" package, offered by the Las Vegas Hilton's "*Startrek: The Experience*" attraction. The vows, which were taken on the couple's fifth wedding anniversary, were made on the bridge of the *Starship Enterprise*.

TOP FIVE
SPACED OUT

1 Orlando, Florida, dentist **Denis Bourguignon** and his entire staff wear *Star Trek* uniforms while working on patients

2 **Britain's David Nutley** is so obsessed with *Star Wars* that he's made his own version. He filmed *Dark Skies* in his spare room and nearby woods for $900

3 *Star Trek* fan **Barbara Adams** of Little Rock, Arkansas, wears her Starfleet Commanding Officer's uniform everywhere she goes —even on jury duty

4 British Trekkie **Tony Alleyne** has turned his apartment into a replica of the Starship Enterprise

5 *Star Trek* fan **Daryl Frazetti** from Boston, Massachusetts, dressed his cat Bones in a Dr. McCoy uniform

Mikel Salsgiver made all the outfits for her Trekkie wedding party.

Holy Roller

"Rolling saint" Lotan Baba makes holy pilgrimages through the Indian countryside by lying on the ground and rolling sideways to his destination. In 1995, he rolled nearly 2,500 mi (4,023 km), averaging between 6 mi (10 km) and 13 mi (21 km) a day. He embarked on a 1,500-mi (2,414-km) roll from India to Pakistan in 2003.

"Rolling Saint" Lotan Baba on a roll in 1994 for world peace, which ended, appropriately, at the Peace Pagoda in Battersea Park, London, England.

Log Jam

The front yards of Bynum, North Carolina, are adorned with wooden figures of dogs, elephants, giraffes, and other animals. They are the work of Clyde Jones who, for more than 20 years, has used his chainsaw to carve out distinctive critters from log stumps. Dozens of his creations stand outside his own house, which was covered in penguins.

ART MADE OUT OF LINT
EXHIBIT NO: 13998
THIS LINT ARTWORK OF JOHN WAYNE IS ACTUALLY LIFE-SIZE, AT 6 FT 4 IN (2 M)

Fowl Play

Armando Parra is a professional chicken-catcher in Key West, Florida, where an estimated 2,000 of the fast-breeding birds run loose in the streets. Armando catches the chickens unharmed, and then they are sent to live on a farm.

How the West was Washed

Slater Barron of Long Beach, California, collects lint from her own laundry, and from that of neighbors and friends, and stores it in color-coded boxes in her studio/garage. She then uses the lint to make pictures of all kinds of people and objects, including this portrait of actor John Wayne, which can be seen in the Ripley's Museum in Hollywood.

U.S.A.
Iowa

One-armed piano players must perform for free.

Royal Flush
Australian Janet Williams is such a fan of the British monarchy that she has "royalty rooms" in her home in Sydney, dedicated to her collection of royal memorabilia.

The Winner by a Nose
Ashrita Furman of New York holds the most world records of any individual, including titles for pogo-stick jumping, brick-carrying, underwater rope-jumping, and sack-racing. In New York in 2004, he also succeeded in pushing an orange for 1 mi (1.6 km) in a time of 24 minutes 36 seconds, using only his nose!

Slap Dash
After years of frustration at finding grammatical errors in newspapers, Jeff Rubin, who runs a newsletter production business, created a new holiday: National Punctuation Day. He hopes that the holiday, which is celebrated every year on August 22, will bring some attention to the widespread problem of poor punctuation.

Full of Beans
In the 1990s, Peggy Gallagher left her job as a paralegal in Chicago to pursue her obsession with Beanie Baby toys. She tracked down rare ones, wrote a book about them, and became a Beanie Baby authenticator—someone who decides if Beanies are genuine.

Grand Slam
Jason Alan Pfaff of Ohio is a man on a mission: To visit every single Denny's restaurant in the world. His website contains reviews of the 200 or more locations he has visited.

The School Run

Author and athlete Sri Chinmoy sponsored a curious endurance race in New York City in 1998. The 3,100-mi (4,989-km) course consisted of running round and round a Queens school between 6 a.m. and midnight for weeks on end. The leading runners completed some 115 laps of the school each day. The winner, Hungary's Istvan Sipos, finished the course in 47 days.

Surf's Up

On February 29, 1976, Dale Webster pledged to surf off the coast of California every day until Leap Day fell again on the fifth Sunday of February. That meant 28 years, or more than 10,000 days of surfing, before he stopped in 2004. He postponed his wedding for ten years, never took a vacation, and took poorly-paid night jobs so that he would be free for surfing.

Stuck on You

Art student Jillian Logue, of Florida, made this senior prom dress and tuxedo entirely out of colored duct tape!

Wash Day Blues?

No stranger to the Ripley's Believe It or Not! television show, Kevin Thackwell, has broken records by attaching 120 clothes pins to his face and neck. Kevin, who is also known as the "Clothes Pin Man," clearly isn't worried about wrinkles.

Casket Case

Casket carver Mark Zeabin from Krestova, British Columbia, makes a line of furniture that will last a lifetime—and then some. For Mark is so keen on coffins that he has designed stereo stands, bars, and even sofa beds that will convert into coffins upon the owner's demise. His theory is that it's a false economy to buy a bookshelf that stores only books when you can have one that will eventually store you too.

Reverse Gear

India's Samir Tandon can sing songs, read newspapers, and repeat entire conversations backward.

Don't Look Back

During the 1930s, Plennie Wingo walked backward around the world! Later he walked backward from LA to San Francisco as part of a Ripley's museum promotion. He always wore mirrored glasses so he could see where he was going.

Tomb Raider
Sara Lock from Suffolk, England, was so enthralled by Ancient Egyptian culture that she turned her spare room into an Egyptian tomb.

White Spirit

In January 2005, 82-year-old Paul Schipper clocked up an incredible 3,903 consecutive days' skiing on Sugarloaf Mountain in Maine, despite the fact that he is almost blind in one eye. From 1981 to 2005, the senior citizen went out skiing every single day that the mountain was open.

Completely Cuckoo

With 561 cuckoo-clocks, Roman Piekarski, proprietor of the Cuckooland Museum in Cheshire, England, has the largest collection of cuckoo-clocks in the world. He dreads Daylight Saving Time, for twice a year it takes him around 12 hours to change all his clocks!

CHRISTMAS CRACKERS!

SOME FOLKS WISH it could be Christmas every day—and for Andy Park it is! Since 1991, Andy, of Wiltshire, England, has been celebrating Christmas on a daily basis.

Andy Park must confuse many people by dressing as "Mr. Christmas" all year round— but he's never short of tinsel to wear.

Every single day, Andy watches the Queen's speech and treats himself to a huge Christmas feast. He calculated that his annual intake is 5,450 turkeys, 18,250 roast potatoes, 43,800 Brussels sprouts, 1,825 turnips,

Faux Fir Tree
Car junk yards are rarely known as scenes of great beauty, but this one in Hamburg, Germany, made an effort to get into the festive spirit for Christmas 2003 by piling its scrap vehicles into the shape of a giant, rusty Christmas tree.

3,650 parsnips, 1,825 pots of cranberry sauce, 7,300 gravy cubes, 7,360 mince pies, and 2,350 Christmas puddings. This is washed down with 8,000 glasses of sherry and 1,560 bottles of Champagne. He has also bought 30 artificial trees, 10,000 balloons, and 33,000 ft (10,058 m) of tinsel. He estimates that his festive fetish has cost him more than £100,000 ($147,500)... not to mention a seriously expanding waistline.

Santa's Little Helpers

Alex Adlam has no shortage of helpers when it comes to preparing Christmas lunch. For his house in Cheltenham, England, is full of hundreds of Santas in all shapes and sizes. Alex is unable to resist any item of Christmas memorabilia, from snowmen and reindeer, to stockings and elves.

His collection of ornaments, plates, cushions, and decorations has turned his home into a grotto. It comes as no surprise that Alex likes to dress for the part, donning a white beard and Santa suit to fit in with his festive surroundings.

Ho, ho, ho! Alex Adlam proudly displays his vast collection of Christmas memorabilia.

TOP FIVE
CELEBRITY PHOBIAS

1 **Madonna**
brontophobia
a fear of thunder

2 **Sid Caesar**
tonsurphobia
a fear of haircuts

3 **Sigmund Freud**
siderodromophobia
a fear of train travel

4 **John Cheever**
gephyrophobia
fear of crossing bridges

5 **Natalie Wood**
hydrophobia
a fear of water
(she died by drowning)

In a Spin
In April 2004, hula hoop performer Alesya Goulevich spun 100 hula hoops simultaneously, at the Big Apple Circus, Boston.

Living Doll

A Maryland couple have raised a Cabbage Patch doll as their only son for 19 years. Pat and Joe Posey treat the 1-ft (0.3-m) doll, christened Kevin, as a human. He "speaks" through Joe, has his own 1,000-sq-ft (93-sq-m) playroom at the couple's home, a full wardrobe and $4,000 of savings for when he goes to college!

Going For a Thong

Since 1996, Russell Doig has gathered more than 4,000 thongs from his local beach near Townsville, Queensland, Australia. Doig combs Alva beach every weekend, scooping up washed-up thongs with a special spike before nailing them to his back fence.

Queen Nefertiti

Forty-year-old schoolteacher Elizabeth Christensen is obsessed with looking like the ancient Egyptian Queen Nefertiti! She has paid over $250,000 for more than 240 operations to change her face to look like a famous ceramic sculpture of the queen.

She Ain't Heavy

An Indian man is carrying his elderly mother on a 17-year-long pilgrimage from their home in northern India to Bangalore in the south. Kailashgiri Brahmachari carries his blind mother in a basket on one shoulder and, in another basket, their belongings. By walking a couple of miles each day, he hopes to reach their destination in 2013.

Big Breakfast

Frank Staley has collected more than 400 breakfast cereal boxes. This is 400 too many for his wife, who has ordered him to move some of them out of their home in Ohio.

Captain Cutlass

As his alter ego, Captain Cutlass, Adrian Collins from Kent, England, organizes and competes in the annual World Plank Walking Championship, held on the Isle of Sheppey. Plankers come from all over the world to take part.

Watching You

During one series of TV's *Big Brother*, Gillian Dutfield of Shropshire, England, lived her life according to the housemates. She cooked the same meals as them, and ate and slept at the same time as them. She even shaved her pet dog with the message to the audience, "Vote for Brian!"

Gnome Home

More than 2,000 garden gnomes and pixies roam free at Ann Atkin's gnome sanctuary in Devon, England. Ann, who is 67, founded the International Gnome Club in 1978. She stoutly defends her lengthy garden-gnome fixation by saying, "I think people form an affinity with them."

Buttery Burial

In "The Popcorn Sarcophagus," the renowned competitive eater, Crazy Legs Conti, was buried alive under 100 cu ft (3 cu m) of popcorn. Breathing through a custom fitted snorkel as he ate, he used colored lights to signal—red meant "danger," green meant "OK," and yellow meant "alert, need more butter!"

Popcorn provided by:

Soil Baron

This U.S. soil collector gathered soil from every single U.S. state. He kept each sample in a small container attached to a map on the spot where it came from.

He's a Barbie Boy

Tony Mattia of Brighton, England, owns more than 1,100 Barbie dolls. He started collecting them in the 1960s. "My parents bought me an Action Man," he says, "but I dressed him up in Barbie's clothes." A Barbie that he bought for $2 (£1) in 1962 is now worth at least $295 (£200). Tony changes the costume of every doll once a month.

Bottle Neck

Indian artist Mayapandi has been painting figures on the insides of bottles for the past six years and hopes eventually to fit 500 in one bottle.

Running on Empties

David Pimm has a collection of more than 10,000 different milk bottles at his home on the Isle of Wight, England.

Navel Gazing

Every day since 1984, Graham Barker from Perth, Australia, has been collecting fluff from his navel. He now has 0.54 oz (16.8 g), which is the world's largest collection.

In For a Penny...

Arizona's Steve Baker is crazy about pennies. He makes skirts, shirts, and bathing suits out of the coins, but his pride and joy is his jumpsuit made out of no fewer than 3,568 of them. It took him 800 hours to make and it weighs 32 lbs (15 kg). Just in case anyone has any doubt as to Steve's obsession, he also drives around in a van covered in 90,000 pennies.

The King and I

Paul MacLeod claims to be Elvis' number one fan—he even called his son Elvis Aaron Presley MacLeod. On show at Graceland Too, his house in Holly Springs, Mississippi, are Elvis' 1951 report card, a gold lamé suit supposedly worn by the King for a 1957 concert, and a casket that plays "Return to Sender," in which Paul plans to be buried.

U.S.A. Connecticut

It is illegal for any beautician to hum, whistle, or sing while working on a customer.

ALL SHOOK UP

- Elvis had an eighth-degree black belt in karate
- Elvis was presented with a special award for helping to sell more popcorn in movie theatres from 1956 to 1957
- Elvis was obsessed with brushing his teeth
- Elvis would wear a football helmet while watching his favorite sport on TV
- 3,166 floral arrangements were delivered to Graceland on the two days following Elvis's death in 1977
- In the Islamic state of Mogadishu, in Somalia, it is illegal to impersonate Elvis without a beard

Sweet on Pez

"They're fun, they're cute, they're small," says Gary Doss, creator of the Burlingame Museum of Pez Memorabilia in California. He's describing Pez candy dispensers —and Gary should certainly know. For, since starting his collection in 1988, he has amassed hundreds of different dispensers, including ones with character heads of Mary Poppins, Mickey Mouse, Batman, and Santa Claus.

Overexposed

Photographer Spencer Tunick is driven by the urge to photograph masses of nude bodies in public places. He favors famous locations, such as New York City's Grand Central Station. Since 1992, he has staged his work on every continent, using up to 7,000 volunteers at once.

Breaking the Mold
Percy Westmore, known as "Perc," amassed a collection of Hollywood personality head molds.

Legal Eagle

In March 2004, 73-year-old Haskell Wexler, of Phoenix, Arizona, was in his 12th year of contesting three $31 parking tickets. The dispute has so far cost him 12 failed lawsuits and almost daily phone calls ($5,000).

The Bottom Line

Over the past 30 years, Barney Smith has painted more than 600 toilet seats, which are on display in his garage in Alamo Heights, Texas.

That Really Sucks

California-based production artist Charlie Lester has been obsessed with vacuum cleaners since early childhood. He has acquired about 140 vintage vacuums (dating from 1905 to 1960) in the past four decades, and is an active member of the Vacuum Cleaner Collectors Club.

Well Done

Nearly 20 years ago, Deborah Henson-Conant got distracted and left a pot of cider on the stove for too long, and was fascinated by the result. Inspired, she decided to create the Burnt Food Museum to showcase all of her culinary disasters. Unfortunately, the museum, which is located in Arlington, Massachusetts, had to be temporarily closed in 2004—due to fire damage.

The Man in Green

"Berney" of Jacksonville, Florida, loved the color green so much that he dressed from head to toe in green, lived in a green house, had green furniture, and owned a restaurant decorated entirely in green.

Do You Take this Superman?

Marcella Encinas was convinced that her husband-to-be, actor Scott Cranford, was her real-life Superman. Therefore, when the couple were looking for a suitable wedding venue in June 2001, they chose Metropolis, Illinois, the self-styled home of Superman, and arranged for Scott to attend the ceremony dressed in full Superman costume. Wonder Woman was the matron of honor, and Robin, Batman's sidekick, was the best man. Among the guests was a dog wearing a cape!

Chain Gang

Stan Willis's life changed forever the moment he bought a small padlock at a flea market in the late 1960s. He began collecting padlocks seriously, before abandoning them in favor of handcuffs. Now Stan, from Cincinnati, Ohio, has more than 900 pairs of handcuffs. Not content with that, he also collects leg irons, restraint chains, fire and police department badges, fire lanterns, and fire helmets.

DINE WITH "THE MAN IN GREEN"
TRADE NAME REG.
FROM RIPLEY'S "BELIEVE IT OR NOT"

SOUTH'S MOST TALKED OF PLACE TO DINE

BAR AND PACKAGE DEPARTMENT

DINING ROOM AND COCKTAIL LOUNGE

Berney's RESTAURANT

BAR AND MIRROR COCKTAIL LOUNGE

JACKSONVILLE FLORIDA

"PEGGY"

A COLORFUL LIFE

JUST AS ACTOR Yul Brynner only wore black for 45 years, so Jean Rath of Santa Maria, California, is obsessed with purple.

She has lilac hair, wears purple clothes, drives only purple cars (with "I Love Purple" bumper stickers), and her business cards and checks name her as "The Purple Lady." She lives in a lavender house, with a lavender mailbox and fence. Of course everything inside is purple too—her violet toilet paper has to be ordered from Canada. Her late husband Bill also wore purple.

Everything in Jean Rath's house has to be purple—unable to buy a fridge or dishwasher in her favorite color, she simply painted them purple.

It's not difficult to see why British folk musician Cresby Brown is known as "Mr Red." He dresses from head to foot in bright scarlet and owns a wealth of red accessories.

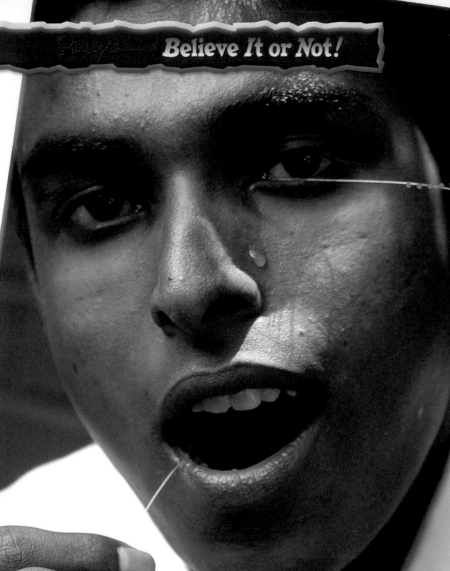

Stringing Us Along
Vijayakanth of India is able to insert a nylon thread through his tear duct and pull it out through his mouth in just 60 seconds.

Carrying the Can
For years, John Milkovisch saved all his old beer cans. He eventually found a use for the can collection: slicing off the tops and bottoms, flattening the sides, and using the metal to cover the exterior of his house in Houston, Texas. He then linked the pull tabs and tops and bottoms of the cans to make curtains, wind chimes, windmills, and sculptures. He even made a beer-can canopy over his driveway and repaired his fence with cans. In 20 years of can construction, he has used more than 39,000 cans.

Shock Treatment
A holy man in northern India touches live electricity wires every day—for kicks. Sadhu Mangal Das, aka "Current Baba," touches a naked wire at least three times a day.

In the Can
Richard Sangster, from the Netherlands, began collecting soft-drinks cans in 1983 and now has more than 10,000, including a German series of Backstreet Boys Pepsi cans.

Book Him!
In 2001, police drove 120 mi (190 km) to LeRoy Anderson's home in Mapleton, Minnesota, brandishing an arrest warrant—because he had forgotten to return two overdue library books.

The Tin Man
This sculpture of a man, made from Coca-Cola tins was made by Teresa Tozer and stands on display at the Ripley's museum in San Francisco.

Ripley's ®
COKE CAN FIGURE
EXHIBIT NO: 15932
CREATED FROM FLATTENED COKE TINS, THIS MALE FIGURE IS LIFE-SIZE

Beyond the Grave
Los Angeles is home to the Virtual Pet Cemetery for Tamagotchis, where bereaved children can go to pay their last respects to their dearly departed virtual friends.

Going by the Wayside
Over a period of 14 years, Fred Smith, a retired lumberjack from Phillips, Wisconsin, sculpted a cast of bizarre characters in concrete. More than 200 of his figures—including cowboys, miners, soldiers, and various animals—still stand by the wayside, and many of them are decorated with beer bottles from Smith's own tavern.

Vintage Fashion
German fashion designer Josefine Edle von Krepl has spent her life collecting old clothes. She has hoarded more than 3,000 garbage can bags full of used garments, many dating back to the 1920s, because she could never bear to throw anything away.

Concrete Proof
Benedictine monk Joseph Zoettel dedicated his life to constructing models of religious landmarks. He spent 50 years making miniature versions of buildings such as the Colosseum and the Vatican. Brother Joseph died in 1961, but 125 of his concrete reproductions are still exhibited at the Ave Maria Grotto at Cullman, Alabama.

Bus Fair
Geoff Price of Walsall, England, has spent the past 44 years collecting toy buses. He has nearly 8,000 models from around the world, and his hobby takes up so much space that he and his wife have been forced to move to a bigger house three times.

Island of the Dolls
For 50 years, Julian Santana scoured the garbage dumps of Mexico City. He was looking for discarded dolls, which he then hung from trees on an island in the city's Teshuilo Lake, where he lived alone. He collected thousands, helped by locals who would take boats to the island and exchange old dolls for the vegetables he grew.

Read All About It
Artist Ronald Max Vollmer produced a unique maze constructed from more than 50,000 old books! Vollmer spent a large part of his life as a scientist but, inspired by his painter father, he always dreamed of becoming an artist. Since the 1990s, he has developed his own style of installation art. One such piece was a trail of lit lamps being carried through his family home. More recently, he embarked on the book maze. Visitors to the maze could wind their way through passages constructed from books stacked high upon one another. Not only could visitors view the piece, but they could also leave their own mark on the installation, by adding their own books if they wished.

Vollmer adds the finishing touches to the 50,000-strong book maze!

A Perfect Match

Prateep Tangkanchanawelekul, from Thailand, has a collection of more than 100,000 matchboxes, including some rare ones. He has even made a jacket out of some of the matchboxes in his collection and claims to wear it wherever he goes.

Magnetic Personality

Over the past 30 years, Louise J. Greenfarb of Las Vegas, Nevada, has collected more than 29,000 fridge magnets, including some featuring portraits of sports heroes, cartoon characters, and presidents. Her ambition is to be buried in her fridge, surrounded by a thousand of her favorite magnets.

In at the Deep End

A Chinese pensioner called Yan performs a daily exercise of walking backward around Bayi Lake because he believes it is good for his health. Unfortunately, in April 2003 he was so busy counting his steps that he lost his bearings, fell in, and had to be rescued by fellow walkers.

Dear Diary...

For no less than four hours a day, every day, from 1972 to 1996, Robert Shields of Dayton, Washington, typed out a record of absolutely everything that had happened to him. His diary, which at 38 million words is thought to be the world's longest, is stored in more than 80 cardboard boxes. An example of his attention to detail is: "July 25, 1993, 7 a.m.: I cleaned out the bath tub and scraped my feet with my fingernails to remove layers of dead skin."

Every Night at the Movies

Derek Atkins of York, England, has visited Odeon cinemas eight times a week since 1988. But he doesn't go to watch the movies—he goes to study the décor. Derek, who used to work for Odeon as an usher and projectionist, admits he is obsessed with the Odeon chain. "If I can't see a film at the Odeon, I won't go to see it at all," he says.

Buzz Off

In 1998, Californian Mark Biancaniello was covered in an estimated 350,000 bees, weighing a total of 87.5 lbs (40 kg).

Gone to Pot

The *Portable Border* installation consisted of 100 plant pots in a line, which stretched as far as 40 ft (12 m). That wasn't all there was to this piece of art, because the flowery line moved approximately 2.5 mi (4 km) through the streets of London, England, during April 2004! British artist Phil Coy simply took the plant at the back of the line and moved it to the front, then took the next plant at the back and moved that to the front, and so on until he eventually reached his destination!

Phil Coy had exhibited his flower art in Germany and Finland, before moving it to the streets of London, England.

Dotty!

KAREN FERRIER IS dotty about spots!

It all started 12 years ago with her Dalmatian dog, Ditto, but now she has a spotted car, spotted clothes, spotted hats, spotted shoes, and a spotted room. She also used to have a spotted motorbike, which she rode in a spotted helmet and spotted leathers. Her remaining ambition is to paint the outside of her house in Southampton, England... with spots, of course.

Spot the Dog

Esther the Dalmatian ran away for three days in October 2003—high-tailing it down a highway, swimming across San Francisco Bay, and running down Runway 28 at San Francisco International Airport.

The Cat's Whiskers

"Stalking Cat," also known as Dennis Avner, a Californian computer repair man, is gradually transforming himself into a feline through painful plastic surgery. "Cat," as he is commonly known, developed his obsession with all things feline at the age of 23, when he had his first tattoo—of tiger stripes. Now 44, "Cat" is covered in striped tattoos. He has even gone so far as to have plastic surgery to give him a cleft lip, synthetic whisker implants, and elongated ears.

Serial Groom

Udaynath Dakshirinay, 80, from Orali, India, has been married no fewer than 90 times. Nobly, he has always chosen poor brides so that he could spread a little of his own wealth. He hopes to clock up a century of wives before he dies.

Splitting Hairs

Leila Cohoon collects hair, but not just any old hair: it must be human hair dating from before 1900. Hair art has been her passion for more than 40 years. Leila's Hair Museum in Independence, Missouri, features jewelry, wreaths, and pictures. Her favorite item is a 19th-century floral tapestry made from the hair of 156 members of one family.

Hair Today...

In the Victorian era, wreaths were made from the hair of a dead person and their relatives. These were placed on the coffin during funeral services and later hung in the family home.

Walmart Worship

Derek's Big Website of Walmart Purchase Receipts was run by Derek Dahlsad of Dilworth, Minnesota. He posted every Walmart receipt he received from 1996 to 2002, and asked visitors to comment on his range of purchases.

Hair Shirt

St. Louis barber Bill Black has made several items of clothing such as dresses, socks, hats, mittens, and even a bikini—from nothing other than human hair!

Ripley's®
HAIR WREATH
EXHIBIT NO: 4897
ORIGINATES FROM THE 1880s AND WAS
PURCHASED BY RIPLEYS IN 1995

Ripley's®
HUMAN HAIR VEST
EXHIBIT NO: 13817
CREATED BY BARBER, BILL BLACK,
MADE ENTIRELY FROM HAIR

Trunk Call

Ever since receiving his first ornamental elephant as a gift from his sister-in-law on his wedding day in 1967, Ed Gotwalt has had a thing about pachyderms. His collection soon grew and his wife suggested he open a museum. Today, Mr. Ed's Elephant Museum in Orrtanna, Pennsylvania, is home to more than 6,000 elephants made from just about every known substance. In his spare time, Ed tours the country selling elephants' favorite food—peanuts!

The Long Way Home

In 2002, a Japanese canoeist finished a 5,965-mi (9,600-km) journey around the country's coast… 23 years after he started! Reiji Yoshioka began his adventure in 1979 from near his home in Kanagawa, and always fitted it in with his work as a printer. He was 64 when he completed the final leg of his trip around the northern island of Hokkaido.

Word Perfect

An Indian man has memorized the entire *Oxford Advanced Learners' Dictionary*. It took Mahaveer Jain just ten months to remember each of the 80,000 individual entries. He can also recall their exact sequence and the page on which they appear.

Beatlemania

Beatle-mad Argentinean Rodolfo Vazquez keeps more than 5,600 items of Fab Four memorabilia in his loft. Among his most treasured possessions are some bricks from the Cavern Club in Liverpool, England, where the Beatles first played.

Salad Days

Radish fanatics can celebrate their devotion to this underrated vegetable every December 23 at the Night of the Radishes exhibition in Oaxaca, Mexico. Huge radishes are carved into highly detailed figures and displayed in intricate scenes that reflect the local culture.

Venerable Beads

Over a period of 13 months, working eight hours a day, Faris Hassan, of Amman, Jordan, used more than 175,000 beads to make a 23-ft (7-m) long rosary.

InDex

ACKNOWLEDGMENTS

Jacket (t/l) Rex Features; (b/l) Erik C Pendzich/Rex Features

4 Erik C Pendzich/Rex Features; 6 (c) Mike Carmichael; 8 (c/l) Ralph Merlino/Rex Features, (b) Nils Jorgensen/ Rex Features; 9 (t, b) Drew Gardner/ Rex Features; 10 (b) SWS/Rex Features; 11 (t/r) Tim Shaffer/Reuters, (b) ZZ/XXD/SPL /Rex Features; 13 Lee Besford/Reuters; 14 (t/r) JZB/Rex Features, (b/l) Dan Charity/ Rex Features; 15 (b) John Gurzinski /AFP/Getty Images; 16 (t/r) Nils Jorgensen/Rex Features; 17 (t/l) Mark Mawson/ Rex Features, (b) Shannon Stapleton/Reuters; 18 (b) Getty Images; 19 (t/l) Alban Donohoe/Rex Features; 20 (b/l) Lindsey Parnaby/Rex Features; 21 (t/r) Action Press/Rex Features, (b/c) ACM/UTN/ZZ/Rex Features; 22 Boston Herald/Rex Features; 23 Eric C Pendzich/Rex Features; 24 (t/l) Simon Jones/Rex Features, (b) Stringer/India/Reuters; 25 (t) Geoff Wilkinson/Rex Features; 27 (t/r) Brendan Beirne/Rex Features, (b) SWS/Rex Features; 28 (t/l) Jagadeesh NV/Reuters; 29 (t/l) Peter Brooker/Rex Features, (b/r) Doug Hall/Rex Features; 30 (t/l) Sukree Sukplang/Reuters, (b/r) Nils Jorgensen/Rex Features; 31 (c) MY/NAP/Rex Features; 33 Ali Jarekji/Reuters.

All other photos are from Ripley's Entertainment Inc.
Every attempt has been made to acknowledge correctly and contact copyright holders and we apologize in advance for any unintentional errors or omissions, which will be corrected in future editions.